Capturing Nature

Capturing Nature

The Writings and Art of
John James Audubon

Edited by Peter and Connie Roop
with Illustrations by Rick Farley

WALKER AND COMPANY

NEW YORK

For Marti and John,
our "natural" friends,
who are wild about birds.

Copyright © 1993 by Peter and Connie Roop
Illustrations © 1993 by Rick Farley

First published in the United States of America in 1993
by Walker Publishing Company, Inc.

Published simultaneously in Canada by Thomas Allen & Son
Canada, Limited, Markham, Ontario

Library of Congress Cataloging-in-Publication Data
Audubon, John James, 1785–1851.
    [Audubon and his journals. Selections]
    Capturing nature: the writings and art of John James Audubon / edited by Peter
and Connie Roop; illustrations by Rick Farley.
        p.   cm.
    Selections from Audubon and his journals.
    Includes bibliographical references.
    Summary: Uses the words of Audubon himself, selected from various sources, to
present an account of the life and work of this nineteenth-century naturalist.
    ISBN 0-8027-8204-3 (C). —ISBN 0-8027-8205-1 (R)
    1. Audubon, John James, 1785–1851—Diaries—Juvenile literature.
2. Birds—North America—Juvenile literature.   3. Naturalists—
United States—Diaries—Juvenile literature.   [1. Audubon, John
James, 1785–1851.   2. Naturalists.   3. Artists.]   I. Roop, Peter.
II. Roop, Connie.   III. Farley, Rick, ill.   IV. Title.
QL31.A9A3   1993
598'.092—dc20
[B]   92-15662
                                                                          CIP
                                                                           AC

Paintings by John James Audubon appear courtesy of the Library of Congress.

Printed in Hong Kong

Set in Weiss
Designed by Virginia Norey

10   9   8   7   6   5   4   3   2   1

Acknowledgments

*J*ohn James Audubon wrote extensively in journals, letters, and books. His granddaughter, Maria Audubon, collected and edited many of his journals. Her two volumes, *Audubon and His Journals*, were our primary sources for the quotations selected for our book. We also enjoyed many hours of looking at Audubon's *Birds of America* pictures, collected in various volumes. To place Audubon in historical perspective we relied on the noted Audubon authority Alice Ford, especially her *Audubon, By Himself* and *John James Audubon*, as well as other authors.

Most of all we delighted in Audubon's own telling of his life and his desire to draw and paint birds "naturally." Through his words and pictures we gained a new appreciation for the natural world, then and now.

John James Audubon was a scientist, storyteller, traveler, businessman, hunter, and writer. Foremost, Audubon was an artistic genius with a vision. He was determined to do what no other artist had done before—to paint birds life-size in their natural habitats, eating, flying, and rearing their young. In doing so, Audubon became one of the world's first naturalists.

From 1803, when he first came to America, until his death in 1851, he spent years wandering the fields, forests, and rivers from Kentucky to Florida, from New Jersey to Montana. Much of what Audubon experienced in those early frontier days has vanished. The billions of Passenger Pigeons that darkened the skies are extinct. Few of the Indians with whom Audubon camped and hunted still live on their native lands. The multitudes of birds he watched and painted can no longer be seen in the very places he walked.

Audubon himself killed thousands of birds for food and study. In Florida he and his companions slaughtered so many birds that they made a pile as large as a small haystack. Yet, as he grew older, Audubon realized that the natural world could not support such wholesale killing. In 1843, after seeing the destruction of hundreds of bison just for their tongues, he wrote, "This cannot last. Even now there is a perceptible difference in the size of the herds, and before many years the Buffalo, like the Great Auk, will have disappeared. Surely this should not be permitted."

Parks across America honor Audubon's achievements as an artist and naturalist. Seven towns in seven states are even named Audubon! The Audubon Society, dedicated to protecting wildlife and

wildlands, is named after this unusual and determined man who struggled and succeeded in telling the world about his beloved birds.

From his own words, we selected these passages to tell Audubon's story of his development into America's foremost bird artist. This is Audubon's personal story as he himself told it.

I Begin Writing My Adventures

On this rainy morning, when I cannot go ashore to hunt, I shall begin to relate some incidents of my life as I drift down the river on a flatboat. I cannot write it all, but if I could, how could I make a little book, when I have seen enough to make a dozen large books?

Hundreds of anecdotes I could relate. It may happen that the pages I am now scribbling over, may hereafter be published.

MARSH HAWK
FALCO CYANEUS
Male Adult 1.   Female Adult 2.   Young Male 3.

My Childhood

My father was Lieutenant Jean Audubon. He sailed as a sea captain to the West Indies, where in 1785 I found light and life in the New World. During my earliest years there and in France he often brought me birds and flowers. With great eagerness he would point out the elegant movements of the birds, and the beauty and softness of their plumage. He called my attention to their shows of pleasure or sense of danger, their perfect forms and splendid attire. He would speak of their departure and their return with the seasons, their haunts, and, most wonderful of all, their change of livery. He excited me to make me study them.

In personal appearance my father and I were of the same height and stature, say about five feet ten inches and with muscles of steel. His manners were those of a most polished gentleman. In temper we much resembled each other also, being warm, irascible, and at times violent. But it was like the blast of a hurricane, dreadful for a time, then calm almost instantly returned.

My mother, an extraordinarily beautiful woman, died shortly after my birth. I was removed to France when only three years old and received by the best of women, Anne Moynet Audubon, my foster mother, and raised and cherished to the utmost of her means.

My stepmother, who was devotedly attached to me—far too much for my good—was desirous that I should be brought up to live and die "like a gentleman," thinking

that fine clothes and filled pockets were the only requisites needful to attain this end. She completely spoiled me, hid my faults, boasted to everyone of my youthful merits, and, worse than all, said frequently in my presence that I was the handsomest boy in France. All my wishes and idle notions were at once gratified.

My father was quite of another mind as regarded my future welfare. He believed not in the power of gold coins as efficient means to render a man happy. He said, "Talents and knowledge, added to sound mental training, assisted by honest industry, can never fail, nor be taken from anyone." Therefore, notwithstanding all my mother's tears, off to school I was sent.

I studied drawing, geography, mathematics, and fencing, as well as music, for which I had considerable talent. Mathematics was hard, dull work. Geography pleased me more. For dancing I was quite enthusiastic.

Because my father was often absent on naval duty, my mother suffered me to do much as I pleased. It is therefore not to be wondered at that, instead of applying myself closely to my studies, I preferred associating with boys of my own age who were more fond of going in search of birds' nests, fishing, or shooting, than studies. Almost every day, instead of going to school, I made for the fields, where I spent my day. My little basket went with me, filled with good eatables, and when I returned home, during winter or summer, it was replenished with curiosities, such as birds' nests, birds' eggs, curious lichens, flowers of all sorts, and even pebbles.

The first time my father returned from sea my room exhibited quite a show, and on entering it he was so

---

HERRING GULL
LARUS ARGENTATUS, Brunn
1. Adult Male Spring Plumage.   2. Young in November
Racoon Oysters

pleased to see my various collections that he complimented me on my taste for such things. But when he inquired what else I had done, and I, like a culprit, hung my head, he left me without saying another word.

One incident of childhood is perfect in my memory . . . one of the curious things that perhaps led me to love birds and finally study them with infinite pleasure. My foster mother had several beautiful Parrots and some monkeys. One monkey was a full-grown male of a very large species. One morning "pretty Polly" asked for her breakfast as usual: "Mignonne wants bread and milk." The monkey walked toward her and killed her. My infant heart agonized at this cruel sight. I begged a servant to beat the monkey, but he refused because he preferred him to the

Parrot. My long and piercing cries brought my mother rushing into the room. I was tranquilized, the monkey forever afterward chained, and Mignonne buried with all the pomp of a cherished one.

During all these years there existed within me a tendency to follow Nature in her walks. Perhaps not an hour of leisure was spent elsewhere than in woods and fields, examining either the eggs, nest, young, or parents of any species of birds. I commenced a series of drawings of the birds of France, which I continued until I had upward of two hundred drawings, all bad enough, yet they were representations of birds, and I felt pleased with them.

As I grew up I was fervently desirous of becoming acquainted with Nature. But the moment a bird was dead, no matter how beautiful it had been in life, the pleasure of possession became blunted for me. I wished to possess all the reproductions of Nature, but I wished to see life in them, as fresh as from the hands of their Maker.

This was impossible. . . . I turned to my father, made known to him my disappointment, and he gave me a book of illustrations that put new life in my veins. Although the pages were not what I longed for, they gave me a desire to copy Nature. To Nature I went and tried to imitate her. But for many years, I saw that my drawings were worse than the ones I regarded as bad in the book.

The worse my drawings were, the more beautiful did the originals appear. To have been torn from the study would have been as death; my time was entirely occupied with art.

I Come to America

Not long after I was seventeen years old, my father, anxious that I should not be enrolled in Napoleon's army, sent me back to my own beloved country, the United States of America. I came with intense and indescribable pleasure.

On landing at New York I caught the yellow fever. The kind man who commanded the ship that brought me from France took charge of me and placed me under the care of two Quaker ladies. To their skillful and untiring care I may safely say I owe my life.

One morning the carriage carried me to Mill Grove, my father's estate in Pennsylvania. Mill Grove was ever to me a blessed spot. The mill was a source of joy, and in the

YELLOW–CROWNED HERON
ARDEA VIOLACEA, L.
Adult Male Spring Plumage 1.
Young in October 2.

cave where the Pewees were wont to build, I never failed to find quietude and delight.

Hunting, fishing, drawing, and music occupied my every moment. Cares I knew not, and cared naught about them. I purchased excellent and beautiful horses, visited all such neighbors as I found in congenial spirits, and was as happy as happy could be.

An anecdote I must relate concerns my ice skating in those early days of happiness. As the world knows nothing of it, I shall give it to you at some length. It was arranged one morning between myself and several other friends of

the same age that we proceed on a duck-shooting excursion up the creek. The ice was in capital order wherever no air holes existed, but of these a great number interrupted our course, all of which we avoided as we proceeded along. The day was spent in much pleasure, and considerable game collected. On our return in the early dusk, I was bid to lead the way. I fastened a white handkerchief to a stick, held it up, and we all proceeded toward home like a flock of wild Ducks going to their roosting ground. Many a mile had been passed, and, as gayly as ever, we were skating swiftly along when darkness came. Now our speed increased. I happened to draw very near a large air hole, and down it I went. My senses left me. I glided with the stream for thirty or forty yards, when, as God would have it, up I popped at another air hole. Here I managed to crawl out. My companions had seen my form suddenly disappear, escaped the danger, and were around me when I emerged from the greatest peril I have ever encountered. I was helped to a shirt from one, a pair of dry breeches from another, and was completely dressed anew. Our line of march continued with much more circumspection. Let the reader, whoever he may be, think as he may like on this singular and, in truth, most extraordinary escape from death. It is the truth.

I Fail at Business

I went to France to obtain my father's consent to marry my neighbor, Lucy Bakewell. My father decided that I should remain some months with him, and to associate me with someone whose commercial knowledge would be of value to me. He joined me with Ferdinand Rozier, and we were fairly smuggled out of France to escape being forced into Napoleon's navy. I went to New York, where I entered as a clerk for Benjamin Bakewell, while Rozier went to a French business in Philadelphia.

SUMMER OR WOOD DUCK
ANAS SPONSA, L.
1, 2. Males. 3, 4. Females.
Platanus occidentalis–Buttonwood Tree

13

The mercantile business did not suit me. The very first venture that I undertook was in indigo. It cost me several hundred pounds, the whole of which was lost. Rozier was no more fortunate than I, for he shipped a cargo of hams to the West Indies, and not more than one-fifth of the cost was returned. Yet I suppose we both obtained a smattering of business.

On April 8, 1808, my Lucy and I were married, and the next morning we left for Louisville, Kentucky. For two years previous to this, Rozier and I had visited the country from time to time as merchants, had thought well of it, and liked it exceedingly.

We floated down the Ohio in a flatboat in company with other young families. We had many goods and

opened a large store at Louisville, which went on prosperously when I attended to it. But birds were birds then as now, and my thoughts were ever toward them as the objects of my greatest delight. I shot. I drew. My days were happy beyond human conception, and beyond this I really cared not. I seldom passed a day without drawing a bird or noting something respecting its habits. Rozier meantime attended to the store counter alone.

When I think of these times and call back to mind the grandeur and beauty of those almost uninhabited shores; when I picture to myself the dense forests that everywhere spread along the hills, unmolested by the ax of the settler; when I see that the vast herds of Elk, Deer, and Buffaloes that once pastured on these hills and in these valleys have ceased to exist; when I reflect that all this grand portion of our Union, instead of being in a state of Nature, is now more or less covered with villages, farms, and towns where the din of hammers and machinery is constantly heard; when I realize that the woods are fast disappearing under the ax by day, and the fire by night; when I think of the hundreds of steamboats gliding to and fro over the whole length of the majestic Ohio; when I see the surplus population of Europe coming to assist in the destruction of the forest, and transplanting civilization into its darkest recesses; when I remember that these extraordinary changes have all taken place in the short period of twenty years—I pause, wonder, and although I know all to be fact, I can scarcely believe its reality. Whether these changes are for the better or for the worse, I shall not pretend to say.

One fine morning I was surprised by the sudden entrance of Mr. Alexander Wilson, the celebrated author of the *American Ornithology*, of whose existence I had never until that moment been apprised. He had two volumes under his arm, and as he approached the table at which I

WHITE−HEADED EAGLE
FALCO LEUCOCEPHALUS, Linn
Male. Yellow Catfish

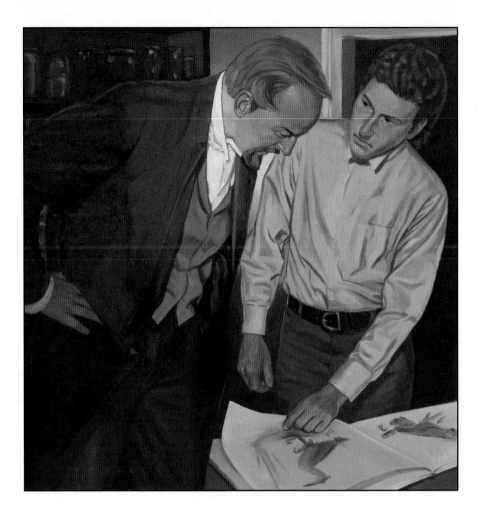

was working, he opened his books, explained the nature of his occupations, and requested my patronage.

I felt surprised and gratified at the sight of his volumes, turned over a few of the plates, and had already taken up his pen to write my name, when my partner rather abruptly said to me in French, "My dear Audubon, what induces you to subscribe to this work? Your drawings are certainly far better, and again, you must know as much of the habits of American birds as this gentleman." Vanity prevented me from subscribing.

Mr. Wilson asked if I had many drawings of birds. I rose, took down a large portfolio, laid it on the table, and showed him as I would show you, kind reader—the whole of the contents—with the same patience with which he had shown me his own engravings.

His surprise appeared great, as he told me he never had the most distant idea that any other individual had been engaged in forming such a collection. He asked me if it was my intention to publish. When I answered no, his surprise seemed to increase. And, truly, such was not my intention. For until a long time after I had not the least idea of presenting the fruits of my labors to the world.

Merchants crowded to Louisville from all our Eastern cities. None of them were, as I was, intent on the study of birds, but all were deeply impressed with the value of dollars. Louisville did not give up on us, but we gave up on Louisville. I could not bear to give the attention required by my business, and which, indeed, every business calls for, and therefore my business abandoned me.

When our boats arrived at Henderson, Kentucky, I purchased a lot of four acres and a cabin. Thomas Bakewell, my brother-in-law, came and joined me in commerce. We prospered for a while, but unfortunately for me, he took it into his brain to persuade me to erect a steam mill. Well, up went the mill at enormous expense, in a country then as unfit for such a thing as it would be now for me to attempt to settle on the moon. The mill was raised and worked very badly. We lost our money.

From this date my difficulties increased. I had heavy bills to pay, which I could not meet. The once wealthy man was now nothing. I gave every particle of property I held to my creditors, keeping only the clothes I wore on that day, my original drawings, and my gun. My Lucy felt the pangs of our misfortunes perhaps more heavily than I but never for an hour lost her courage. Her brave and cheerful spirit accepted all, and no reproaches from her beloved lips ever wounded my heart. With her was I not always rich?

I Become an Artist

One of the most extraordinary things among all these adverse circumstances was that I never for a day gave up listening to the songs of our birds, or watching their peculiar habits, or delineating them in the best way I could. Nay, in my deepest troubles, I frequently would wrench myself from the persons around me and retire to some secluded part of our noble forests.

Finally I paid every bill. My plantation in Pennsylvania had been sold and nothing was left to me but my humble talents. Were those talents to remain dormant? Was I to

see my beloved Lucy and children suffer and want bread in the abundant state of Kentucky? Was I inclined to cut my throat in foolish despair? No! I *had* talents, and to them I instantly resorted.

To be a good draftsman was to me a blessing. To any other man, be it a thousand years hence, it will be a blessing also. I at once undertook to make portraits of the human head in black chalk and succeeded admirably. I commanded exceedingly low prices but raised these prices as I became known in this capacity. I was sent for miles to take likenesses of persons on their deathbeds.

My drawings of birds were not neglected meantime. In this there seemed to hover around me almost a mania. I would even give up doing a head, the profits of which would have supplied our wants for a week, to represent a citizen of the feathered tribe. I now drew birds far better than I had ever done before misfortune intensified my abilities.

When, as a lad, I first began my attempts at representing birds on paper, I was far from possessing much knowledge of their nature. Like hundreds of others, I was under the impression that it was a finished picture of a bird because it possessed some sort of head and tail, and two sticks in lieu of legs. What bills and claws I drew, to say nothing of a perfectly straight line for a back, and a tail stuck in anyhow, like an unshipped rudder.

Many persons saw my miserable attempts and praised them to the skies. Perhaps no one was ever nearer being completely wrecked than I by these mistaken though affectionate words. My father, however, spoke very differently to me. He constantly impressed upon me that nothing in the world possessing life and animation was easy to imitate, and he hoped I would become more and more alive to this. He was so kind to me and so deeply interested in my improvement that to have listened carelessly

BLACK–HEADED GULL
LARUS ATRICILLA, L.
Adult Male Spring Plumage 1. Young First Autumn 2.

to his serious words would have been highly ungrateful. I listened less to others, more to him, and his words became my law.

One day, while watching the habits of a pair of Pewees, I looked so intently at their graceful attitudes that a thought struck my mind like a flash of light. Nothing, after all, could ever answer my enthusiastic desires to represent Nature except to copy her in her own way, alive and moving. Then I began again. On I went, forming hundreds of outlines of my favorites, the Pewees. How

BELTED KINGFISHER
ALCEDO ALCYON, Linn
Male 1,2. Female 3.

24

good or bad I cannot tell. I continued for months, simply outlining birds as I observed them, either alighted or on the wing, but could finish none of my sketches. I procured many individuals of different species, tried to place them in such attitudes as I had sketched. But, alas! They were dead, to all intents and purposes, and neither wing, leg, nor tail could I place according to my wishes.

A second thought came to my assistance. By means of threads I raised or lowered a head, wing, or tail, and by fastening the threads securely, I had something like life before me; yet much was wanting. When I saw living birds, I felt blood rush to my temples, and almost in despair I spent about a month without drawing but deep in thought, and daily in the company of the feathered inhabitants.

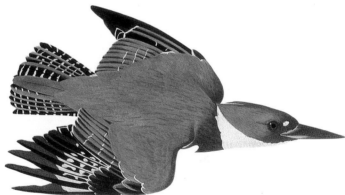

One morning I leapt out of bed and rode off at a gallop to Norristown. I entered the first opened shop, inquired for wire of different sizes, bought some, jumped on my steed, and was soon again at Mill Grove. The wife of my tenant, I really believe, thought I was mad, as, on offering me breakfast, I told her I only wanted my gun. I was off to the creek and shot the first Kingfisher I met. I picked the bird up and carried it home by the bill. I pierced the body of the fishing bird and fixed it to a board. Another wire, passed above his upper mandible, held the head in a pretty fair attitude, while smaller ones fixed the feet according to my notions. The last wire proved a delightful elevator to the bird's tail, and at last, there stood before me the *real* Kingfisher. This is what I shall call my first drawing actually from nature, for even the eye of the Kingfisher was as if full of life whenever I pressed the lids aside with my finger.

As I wandered, mostly bent on the study of birds, and with a wish to represent all those found in our woods, to the best of my powers, I gradually became acquainted with their forms and habits. The use of my wires was improved by constant practice. Whenever I produced a better representation of any species the preceding one was destroyed.

My drawings at first were made altogether in water-colors, but they wanted softness and a great deal of finish. For a long time I was much dispirited at this, particularly when vainly endeavoring to imitate birds of soft and downy plumage, such as that of most Owls, Pigeons, Hawks, and Herons. A so-called accident came to my aid.

One day, after having finished a miniature portrait of the one dearest to me in all the world, a portion of the face was injured by a drop of water, which dried where it fell. I labored a great deal to repair the damage, but the blur still remained. I took a piece of colored chalk, applied the pigment, rubbed the place with a cork stump, and at once produced the desired effect.

My drawings of Owls and other birds of similar plumage were much improved by such applications. I have continued the same style ever since.

NIGHT HERON OR QUA BIRD
ardea Nycticorax, l.
Adult 1. Young 2.

I Publish Birds of America!

In 1826, America having by now become my country, I prepared, and with deep sorrow, to leave it for England, after having tried in vain to publish in the United States. I knew not an individual in England. My situation appeared precarious in the extreme. I left my dear Lucy and my two sons as Lucy was unwilling to abandon her work as a private teacher. She was earning enough income so she generously offered to help forward my aim of publication.

On the 17th of May, the *Delos* put out to sea. I was immediately affected with sea-sickness, which, however, lasted but a short time. I remained on deck constantly, forcing myself to exercise.

SNOWY OWL
STRIX NYCTEA, Linn
Male 1. Female 2.

One day I caught four Dolphins; how much I have gazed at these beautiful creatures, watching their last moments of life, as they changed their hue in twenty varieties of richest arrangement of tints, from burnished gold to silver bright, mixed with touches of ultramarine, rose, green, bronze, royal purple, quivering to death on our hard broiling deck. As I stood and watched them, I longed to restore them to their native element in all their original strength and vitality; and yet I felt but a few moments before a peculiar sense of pleasure in catching them with a hook to which they were allured by false pretenses.

As I approached the coast of England I felt no pleasure, and were it not for the sake of my Lucy and my children, I would have readily embarked the next day to return to America.

But I was received by the most notable people in and around Liverpool. The engraver William Lizars offered to bring out my *Birds of America* in the size of life.

My plan was to publish one number at my own expense and risk and, with it under my arm, make my way throughout England. If I could procure three hundred good substantial names of persons or associations or institutions, I could not fail doing well for my family. But to do this, I underwent many sad perplexities and perhaps never again would have—certainly not for many years—seen my beloved America or my family.

I finished the two first years of publication, the two most difficult years I encountered. I could not publish more than five pictures annually, because it would make too heavy an expense to my subscribers and required more workmen than I could find in London. The work, when finished, would contain eighty pictures; therefore, I had seventy more to issue, which would take fourteen years more. It was a long time to look forward to, but it could not be helped.

I was sorry that some of my friends were against the pictures being the size of life. I must acknowledge it rendered the work rather bulky, but my heart was always bent on it, and I could not refrain from attempting it. I accompanied the descriptions of the birds with many anecdotes and accounts of localities connected with the birds themselves and with my travels in search of them.

The work is equal to anything in the world at present. I superintended the engraving and coloring personally. I prayed that my courage would not fail. My industry I knew would not. This is what I tried. If I did not succeed I could return to my woods and there in peace and quiet live and die.

To Britain I owe nearly all of my success. She furnished the house of artists and engravers, R. Havell & Son, through which my labors have been presented to the world. She has also granted me the highest patronage and honors. To Britain, I shall ever be grateful.

I Return to My Beloved America

$\mathcal{N}$ow that my book was a success I made up my mind to return to America. My business was as well arranged for as possible. I collected some money, paid all my debts, and took my passage. I sailed on April 1, 1829. The voyage was uneventful, and America was reached on May 1.

AMERICAN CROW
CORVUS AMERICANUS
Male.   Black Walnut.
Nest of the ruby-throated Hummingbird

Immediately I began the search for new birds for the continuation and completion of the *Birds of America*. I wished to devote every moment to drawing such birds and plants that would give my publication the degree of perfection of that portion already published.

I wish I had eight pairs of hands, and another body to shoot the specimens. I am delighted in my drawings this season of 1829. Forty-two drawings in four months, eleven large, eleven middle size, and twenty-two small. I rise long before day and work till nightfall, when I take a walk and go to bed.

I close this now, knowing I am a poor writer; I can scarcely manage to scribble a tolerable English letter. I know that I am not a scholar, but meantime I am aware that no man living knows better than I do the habits of our birds. No man living has studied them as much as I have done. With the assistance of my old journals and

books, which were written on the spot, I have at least put down plain truths that may be useful and perhaps interesting.

I cannot help but think a curious event is this life of mine.

GREEN HERON
ARDEA VIRESCENS, L.
Adult Male 1. Young in September 2.

38

Source Notes

$\mathscr{O}$ur selections, with minor editing, come from Maria Audubon (1986), *Audubon and His Journals*, vols. 1, 2. New York: Dover Publications (reprint of original published by Scribner's Sons, New York). These passages reflect our understanding and interpretation of Audubon's artistic development based on our extensive reading. Our other sources include:

Adams, Alexander (1966). *John James Audubon, A Biography*. New York: G. P. Putnam's Sons.

Durant, Mary, and Harwood, Michael (1980). *On the Road with John James Audubon*. New York: Dodd, Mead.

Ford, Alice (1969). *Audubon, by Himself*. New York: Natural History Press.

Ford, Alice (1964). *John James Audubon*. Norman: University of Oklahoma Press.

Ford, Alice (1951). *Audubon's Animals*. New York: Studio-Crowell.

Howard, Joan (1954). *The Story of John James Audubon*. New York: Grosset & Dunlap.

Lindsey, Alton, ed. (1985). *The Bicentennial of John James Audubon*. Bloomington: Indiana University Press.